This book was written by

_____

D1114388

Dad, I wrote this book for you because

I am the little dinosaur and you

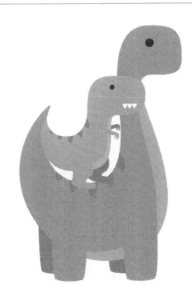

My name is

_____

_____

and I am

_____

years old.

My dad's name is

and he is

years old.

We all had so much fun when we went to

I like it when you tell me that I am

I want you
to know that
you are

My favorite thing to do in the world is

When I need help with

_____

_____

_____

_____

_____

_____

, I ask my dad.

I inherited

_____

_____

_____

_____

_____

from my dad.

My dad makes me laugh when

My dad's perfect father's day would be

My dad and I

when we spend
time together.

I show my dad how much I love him by

My dad is the kind of person that

My favorite memory with my dad is

I know my dad likes being a father because

Something not many people know about my dad is

_____

_____

_____

_____

I was upset but dad made me feel better by

When I get older, I hope my dad and I

A good father should always

Dads are
special because

When I was little, I always felt good when

Dad, you are my hero because

If my dad was a superhero, his power would be

I admire my dad because

When I think of my dad, I think of

My dad knows how to

better than anyone!

When dad was a little dinosaur like me, he

My dad always tells me the story of the time

What is a dad supposed to do?

My dad is
special because

A good father should always

Something special I can do for my dad on father's day is

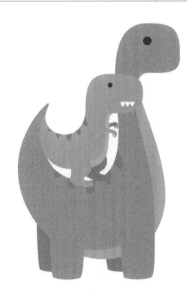

My dad is the kind of person that

The most important thing a dad can do is

People who know my dad, say he

My dad is so proud of me when I

I love my dad
because

When I grow up, I want to be

just like my dad!

I remember the time when dad and I

How can I show my dad I appreciate him?

My dad is really good at

My earliest memory of my dad is

On father's day, I want my dad to know

_____

_____

_____

_____

_____

The most important lesson dad taught me is

My dad's hair is

and his eyes are

My dad's work is

My favorite food is

and my dad's is

The hardest part of being a father is

My favorite game is

And my dad's favorite thing to do is

I wrote you this poem called
My Dad Is

Dad.
Thank you.
For everything.